Contents

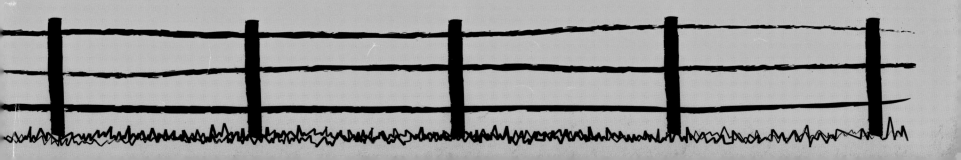

Meet the horses

Neigh! The sun rises over

the field. Here come the horses!

They gallop with their strong legs.

Their hoofs beat the ground.

Horses have wide-set eyes,

pointed ears and large nostrils.

Horses see, hear and smell

very well.

Horses can be bay, black, grey
or many other colours.
A golden horse is called a
palomino. Horses might have
spots or other markings.

Horses are measured from the

ground to their shoulders.

The biggest horses can be taller

than 1.8 metres (6 feet).

That's taller than a minivan!

Time to eat

Horses eat grass, hay and grain.

They drink water from ponds,

streams or tanks.

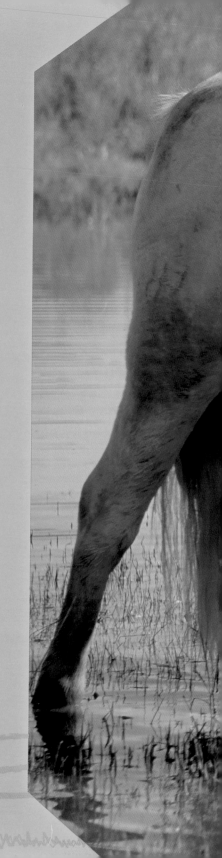

New life

A foal is born! It stands up just hours after birth. Females grow up to be mares. Males are called geldings or stallions.

Horses can live for 30 years.

Horses in action

People raise horses for many reasons. Draught horses, such as Percherons, can pull heavy loads. In places like Canada and the United States, horses help move cattle on ranches.

People ride horses in races,

in shows and on trails.

Thoroughbreds are fast racehorses.

Arabians are best for long

distance riding.

Time to rest

Some horses sleep in fenced pastures.

Other horses rest in stalls

inside stables or barns.

Stall floors are padded with straw

or sawdust to make a soft bed.

Glossary

bay reddish-brown, with a black mane and tail

cattle group of cows raised for their meat

foal young horse

gallop fastest movement or run of a horse

gelding male horse that can't be used for breeding

grain foods like oats, corn and barley

hoof hard part of a horse's foot

mare female horse after she turns four years old

nostril opening in the nose

pasture land where farm animals eat grass and exercise

show contest with many events

stall small room inside of a stable or barn

stallion adult male horse

Read more

A Horse's View of the World (Pet Perspectives), Flora Brett (Capstone Press, 2016)

Farm Animals (World of Farming), Nancy Dickmann (Raintree, 2011)

Horses and Ponies (Animal Family Albums), Paul Mason (Capstone Raintree, 2013)

Websites

discoverykids.com/category/animals/
Learn facts about animals and check out photos of all sorts of animals on this website.

kids.nationalgeographic.com/animals
Search for different sorts of animals and learn where they live, what they eat and more.

Index